GOD AT WORK
COURSE

Living every day with purpose

GUEST MANUAL

CONTENTS

INTRODUCTION

Welcome to the *God at Work* course. Finding purpose in the work we do is one of the greatest challenges we face. The *God at Work* course aims to equip Christians, and those interested in learning more about the Christian faith, to find purpose in every aspect of their working lives.

Over six sessions, the course provides a Christian perspective on how to face challenges at work, as well as teaching on how to support our family and friends in the difficulties we all inevitably face.

We hope you enjoy the course!

SESSION 1

Work Matters

WELCOME

The course is aimed at:

- those in paid employment
- those working in the voluntary sector
- those who work but are not paid (eg, stay-at-home parents)
- those who are between jobs
- those currently not working, but who hope to work in the future (eg, students)

PURPOSE

Finding purpose in our work is one of the greatest challenges we face.

COURSE OVERVIEW

Six key areas:

1. Work Matters
2. Ambition and Life Choices
3. Tough Decisions
4. Stress and Work-Life Balance
5. Failure, Disappointment and Hope
6. Money and Giving

GOD WORKS

Throughout scripture God is described as:

- a gardener
- an artist
- a potter
- a shepherd
- a king
- a home-maker and
- a builder

'O Lord, how manifold are your works!' (Psalm 104:24).

Jesus said 'My Father is still working, and I also am working' (John 5:17).

EXERCISE 1

Discuss in small groups:

- What do you do for work?
- What might prevent a Christian from taking their faith into the workplace?

THEOLOGY OF WORK

1. THE TRINITY

'Now the earth was formless and empty, darkness was over the surface of the deep, and the Spirit of God was hovering over the waters' (Genesis 1:2).

2. CREATION

i. God works to create the world
ii. Adam works in the Garden of Eden (Genesis 2:15)
iii. Creation Mandate (eg, Jeremiah 29)

3. THE INCARNATION

Jesus came to earth with a job to do.

Jesus declares, 'My Father is always at his work to this very day, and I, too, am working' (John 5:17).

4. THE CROSS AND THE RESURRECTION

Jesus' resurrected body was raised up, transformed and glorified (1 Corinthians 15:3-4).

'...you know that your labour in the Lord is not in vain' (1 Corinthians 15:58).

5. JESUS' RETURN TO HEAVEN

Our prayers are heard.

6. PENTECOST

Christ's promised gift of the Holy Spirit

- on the day of Pentecost (Acts 2)
- today

KINGDOM WORK

The Kingdom of God = the 'sphere of God's goodness and rule' on the earth.

Sometimes our work is *fruitful*, and at other times can seem *futile*.

Colossians 3:23: 'Whatever you do, work at it with all your heart, as working for the Lord, not for human masters...'

Hebrew word for 'work' (*avodah*) is the same word for 'worship'.

Let us be able to say that our work-station is also our worship-station.

EXERCISE 2: WHY DO YOU WORK?

Answer the question on your own and then discuss in your small group.

'Why do you work?'

Tick the three answers that matter the most to you.

- ☐ to earn money and to enjoy life
- ☐ for personal satisfaction and success
- ☐ to bring about some social good
- ☐ to enjoy relationships and friendships with colleagues
- ☐ to evangelise and share my faith
- ☐ other (explain)

PURPOSE

Jesus' work was aligned with that of the Father. We need to identify the role that God has specifically called us to. When we do this, our work is infused with purpose.

Reasons/purposes why God may have placed you in your current job:

1. To be a responsible steward

2. Earn money to give away to mission and the church

3. To earn your own money to support yourself and your family (1 Thessalonians 4)

4. To be a positive influence for God in a negative environment (see Jeremiah 48:11-12)

5. To share the Gospel with your colleagues

6. To be a listening ear for your colleagues

Primary responsibility – to do the job we are paid to do!

HOLY JOBS

So-called 'sacred-secular divide'.

Bishops and bankers, nuns and nurses can have holy jobs!

PASTOR
▼
Missionary
▼
Full-time church worker
▼
Tentmaker
▼
Elder
▼
Deacon
▼
Church member
▼
Poor Christian
▼
Middle Income Christian
▼
Rich Christian

GOD
▼ ▼ ▼ ▼ ▼ ▼ ▼
Pastor Missionary Church worker Tentmaker Elder Deacon Member

Adapted from the illustration in *Thank God It's Monday*, Mark Greene (Scripture Union Publishing, Third Edition: 2001), page 18.

Abraham was a cattle trader; Joseph was Prime Minister; Luke was a doctor; the first Ethiopian convert was a central banker; Dorcas was in fashion; Simon the tanner was the Louis Vuitton of his day; and Jesus was a carpenter.

Paul uses the same word for 'manual labour' as he does for 'Christian work'.

EXERCISE 3: GOD'S PURPOSE FOR OUR WORK

Discuss the following questions in your small groups and pray together at the end about any issues or questions that come up:

- What is your job now; what is your current sphere of influence in it?
- What are you passionate about?
- What may God be calling you to do in the job you are currently in?
- Have you felt God speak to you about your job in the past?
- Pray for God to show you your purpose in your current job

HOMEWORK/GOING DEEPER

At home, pray through the questions in Exercise 3, asking God to help you discern what he may be saying about your purpose in your current work situation.

ACTION PLAN

Use this space to write down anything you would like to follow up on as a result of this session.

SESSION 2

Ambition and
Life Choices

CHRISTIAN AMBITION

'The passionate and contented pursuit of challenging yet attainable God-given objectives.'

- **Passionate**, '...it is God who works in you to will and to act according to his good purpose' (Philippians 2:13)
- **Contented**
- **Challenging**, 'Do not settle for black and white if God has given you a vision in colour' (Revd John Collins)
- **Attainable**
- **God-given**, how do we make career choices?
- **Relationships**, our main reference point should be our relationship with God, which is developed through regular prayer and reading the Bible

EXERCISE 1

This exercise aims to help us think about when we can read the bible or pray during the day. In the table below, tick the times when you could read the Bible or pray.

Time of day	Bible reading	Praying
Before breakfast		
Whilst running or at the gym		
Whilst commuting in the morning		
After the school run		
At my desk first thing		
During my lunch break		
Whilst commuting in the evening		
Before dinner		
After dinner		
With my partner just before bed		
In bed		
Other		

'The Lord confides in those who fear him; he makes his covenant known to them' (Psalm 25:14).

STEPPING OUT IN FAITH

Pray then act.

'Whether you turn to the right or to the left, your ears will hear a voice behind you, saying, "This is the way; walk in it"' (Isaiah 30:21).

ADVICE FROM OTHERS

Talk through options with trusted, mature Christian friends.

Consider God's timing – you cannot squeeze a fruit ripe. 'I am the Lord; in its time I will do this swiftly' (Isaiah 60:22).

We are not just called out of situations but into new openings and challenges, '...retain the place in life that the Lord has assigned you and to which God has called you' (1 Corinthians 7:17).

SIGNS

Gideon laid a fleece before the Lord to test a decision (Judges 6:36-40).

The fleece was laid after the decision had been made.

HOW TO ACHIEVE YOUR AMBITIONS

Start with the end in mind.

'I make known the end from the beginning' (Isaiah 46:10).

Split long-term goals into shorter-term ones.

Moses speaks about The Promised Land: 'The Lord your God will drive out those nations before you, little by little. You will not be allowed to eliminate them all at once, or the wild animals will multiply around you. But the Lord your God will deliver them over to you' (Deuteronomy 7:22-23).

'All things work together for good' (Romans 8:28, American KJV).

'Do not conform any longer to the pattern of this world, but be transformed by the renewing of your mind. Then you will be able to test and approve what God's will is—his good, pleasing and perfect will' (Romans 12:2).

EXERCISE 2

The purpose of this exercise is to find out what motivates us at work. Do this on your own and then discuss in small groups.

What drives you to do well at work? Put the motivations listed below in order from 1 to 10, with 1 being what drives you the most, and 10 being what drives you the least.

- ■ Service
- ■ Money
- ■ Promotion
- ■ Status / Recognition
- ■ Fulfilment
- ■ Challenge
- ■ Competition
- ■ Winning
- ■ Success
- ■ Teamwork
- ■ Other (describe)

_____
_____
_____
_____
_____
_____
_____
_____

DESTRUCTION AND DECEPTION – HOW TO RECOGNISE THE DANGERS

Lives can be destroyed by ambition that gets out of control.

'The heart is deceitful above all things' (Jeremiah 17:9).

Listen to the Holy Spirit.

Be accountable.

EXERCISE 3: THE 'AMBITION AUDIT'

Exercise 3 can help us recognise if our ambitions are destructive. Complete the 'Ambition Audit' by ticking one answer for each of the questions given.

	Agree strongly	Agree	Neither agree nor disagree	Disagree	Disagree strongly
Are you suspicious of others at work?					
Are you satisfied when others fail?					
Do you like talking about/ gossiping about others?					
Do you find it hard to receive advice from other people?					
Do you feel that you know best about your own ambition?					
I am not satisfied with my current job					

Now add up your score:

5 points for every 'Agree strongly' answer

4 points for every 'Agree' answer

3 points for every 'Neither agree nor disagree' answer

2 points for every 'Disagree' answer

1 point for every 'Disagree strongly' answer

Total: ....

Results:

Score 30 to 21 – you may be gripped by a degree of selfish ambition.

Score 20 to 16 – a generally healthy attitude to ambition, but no room for complacency.

Score 15 to 6 – it is likely that you currently have no problems with selfish ambition.

Helpful questions for career direction:

1. Do I have confidence whilst praying and worshipping that God is setting the agenda or are there persistent niggles?
2. Is my ambition so personal that I don't want to talk about it with others?

PERSEVERANCE

Jesus was ambitious to complete the work that God had sent him to do (John 4:34).

His last cry on the cross was, 'It is finished' (John 19:30).

Paul strained towards the goal God had given him and could say he had 'fought the good fight' and had 'finished the race' (2 Timothy 4:7).

HOMEWORK/ GOING DEEPER

At home, spend some time thinking and praying about the following questions:

- What are your long-term goals for work?
- How can you split them into shorter-term goals?
- Spend time reassessing your own calling, and asking yourself if your ambitions are truly aligned with the purpose that God has given you
- If you know that you find it difficult to persevere, think about how you might increase your own perseverance in the right job

EXERCISE 4

Why do we sometimes find it hard to stick at the job that we have been called to? Fill in the grid below ticking the degree to which each statement applies to you.

Reason	Applicability None	Applicability Low	Applicability Medium	Applicability High
Boredom/ Monotony				
Can't see purpose in it				
Burnt out/ tired				
Difficult relationships at work				
Don't feel competent at job				
Find it hard to live out faith at work				
Performance targets always set too high to meet				
Other reason(s)				

NOTES

SESSION 3

Tough Decisions

A BIBLICAL FRAMEWORK FOR MAKING TOUGH DECISIONS

EXERCISE 1

Discuss in small groups:

- Identify one tough decision you have made in the past related to a work situation
- How did you go about making the decision?
- What steps did you take before deciding what to do?

DECISION-MAKING

A process. Four aspects:

1. SCRIPTURE

Aligned with God's word.

2. REASON

'Come now, let us reason together' (Isaiah 1:18).

3. CONSCIENCE

St Augustine described it as 'a kind of silent clamour of truth ringing inside'. The Holy Spirit guides us through our conscience.

4. CONSEQUENCES

Think about the affect of the decision on other areas of life.

The best decisions are made when these four aspects are aligned.

DECISIONS AND VALUES

Integrity means that our decisions should be aligned with our values.

EXERCISE 2

First, on your own, identify one tough decision you are currently facing, but which you have not made yet. (If you are not facing a tough decision at present, think about a potential issue that may come up in the future instead.)

- Try to 'make the complex simple' by writing down the issue using the minimum amount of words possible
- Consider the four aspects – Scripture, Reason, Conscience and Consequences. Consider how each of these speak to the situation you are facing
- Think about how you might make the best decision in light of the above

Discuss each aspect of making the decision in your small group and pray for God's guidance as you go forward.

HOW TO MAKE WISE CHOICES

When faced with possible conflict, what should we do?

- avoid it
- cut a deal
- make a stand

EXERCISE 3

Case Study: read the workplace scenario below and then discuss in small groups what you would do in this situation.

'You've been asked to give a presentation to the boss of your boss on the project that your team is currently working on. The project requires investment from the business in order to survive and for the team to continue. You do some thorough research and predict the amount of business that you think the project will deliver. Your boss sees the projections before the presentation, and although he is impressed by your research, says the size of the project is not big enough and tells you to double the numbers. What do you do?'

Then read Daniel 1:3-16.

FIVE STEPS FOR MAKING WISE CHOICES

1. LISTEN TO THE QUESTION

Questions Jesus faced:

i. Luke 20:2-7 — not every question has to be answered

ii. Luke 20:21-25 — we do not have to restrict our answers to the options offered

iii. Luke 20:27-33 — when the real purpose of the question is to elicit a straight answer, then one should be given

2. MAKE THE COMPLEX SIMPLE

Write down the issue using the minimum number of words.

3. FOLLOW THE WISDOM OF GOD

Wisdom is knowing and doing what is right and what comes from God.

Step back, take time out to seek God.

4. CONSIDER THE CONSEQUENCES

Take a long view. Jesus says, 'Suppose one of you wants to build a tower. Will he not first sit down and estimate the cost to see if he has enough money to complete it?' (Luke 14:28)

Assess the risk. 'You will keep in perfect peace him whose mind is steadfast, because he trusts in you' (Isaiah 26:3)

Ask for advice and pray with trusted Christian friends.

5. IMPLEMENT THE STRATEGY

Called to be 'as shrewd as snakes and as innocent as doves' (Matthew 10:16).

Daniel 1.

HOMEWORK/GOING DEEPER

Think about your values. List three or four values that you would like to work by consistently, both in and out of the workplace. Share these with another person and pray for God's help to live them out.

NOTES

SESSION 4

Stress and Work-Life Balance

IMPLICATIONS OF STRESS

The study revealed that stress at work puts the same strain on the heart as being forty pounds overweight.

Prolonged bouts of tension have the same effect on blood pressure as ageing thirty years.

Those who suffer stress often have trouble sleeping, or report waking up in the night worrying about work.

Psychological side effects:

- Inability to concentrate for a sustained period of time
- Irrational fear or aggression towards colleagues
- Feeling overwhelmed
- Feeling guilty when we are not working

Stress strangles our relationships with other people and with God.

Parable of the Sower (Mark 4:1-20).

* It is worth noting that if you are suffering from severe stress it may be wise to consider seeing your doctor, or taking some time off work to rest and recover.

FOOLISH APPROACHES

1. Denial

2. Pretending stress is good

STRESS VS PRESSURE

Not the same.

Stress is our own adverse reaction to excessive pressure.

EXERCISE 1: WHAT IS MOST STRESSFUL ABOUT YOUR JOB?

Share your answer to this question with your small group. Also decide where you would put yourself at the moment on the 'Pressure/Performance Curve'.

THE PRESSURE/PERFORMANCE CURVE

Performance

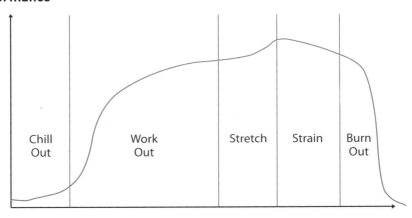

Chill Out   Work Out   Stretch   Strain   Burn Out

Level of Pressure

DEALING WITH STRESS

I. INTERNAL APPROACH

This approach focuses on how we can limit any adverse, internal reaction we may have to the external pressure that we face.

Jesus experienced stress. Eg: the garden of Gethsemane, or the day recorded in Luke 8:22-56.

SEVEN BIBLICAL STRATEGIES

1. STAY HEALTHY

Our body is a temple of the Holy Spirit (1 Corinthians 6:19).

2. PRAY AND READ THE BIBLE

Pray at all times (Philippians 4:6).

Know the Scriptures (2 Timothy 3:15-17).

3. FIGHT FEAR

Those who trust 'will have no fear of bad news; their hearts are steadfast, trusting in the Lord' (Psalm 112).

Ask God for the peace of the Holy Spirit (John 14:27).

4. TAKE JOY SERIOUSLY

'Be joyful always' (1 Thessalonians 5:16).

5. TAKE AN EMOTIONAL BREAK

Jesus often withdrew for 'mini-breaks' throughout his ministry, (see John 6:15 for an example).

Rick Warren has said, 'Divert daily, withdraw weekly, abandon annually.'

6. TAKE CONTROL OF OUR THOUGHTS

'Finally, brothers, whatever is true, whatever is noble, whatever is right, whatever is pure, whatever is lovely, whatever is admirable—if anything is excellent or praiseworthy—think about such things' (Philippians 4:8).

7. MINISTER IN THE OPPOSITE SPIRIT

Paul's example
1 Corinthians 4:12-13.

II. EXTERNAL APPROACH: ACHIEVING WORK-LIFE BALANCE

Another approach to dealing with stress is to try to influence the external pressures placed upon us.

PREVENTATIVE

Set the right priorities.

Get enough rest.

Respect the Sabbath (Isaiah 28:11-13).

COMPULSIONS AND ADDICTIONS

We can be slaves to habits and attitudes that affect the way we live our lives.

MANAGE PRIORITIES, NOT TIME

God knows the bigger picture.

Jesus waits two days to heal Lazarus (John 11:1-16).

EXERCISE 2

Fill out the grid by ticking the box that shows the extent to which each issue applies to your life. Share the top issue with someone in your small group.

Bad habit / Attitude	Applicability None	Applicability Low	Applicability Medium	Applicability High
Workaholism				
Lust for money				
Unforgiveness				
Anger				
Lying				
Substance abuse				
Pornography				
Eating extremes				
Unfaithfulness				
Power seeking				
Identity in appearance				
Identity in being in relationships				
Identity in consuming (shopping/ materialism)				
Irrational fear				
Other (describe)				

IDOLS

Idols are anything that push God out of our lives. Workaholism can become an idol.

FREEDOM AND DISCIPLINE – HOW TO GET THE TREND LINE RIGHT

The short-term breakdown of time spent between work, family and God is not important, rather it is the longer-term trend that matters.

DIARY REVIEWS

ANNUAL DIARY REVIEW

Look back at the past year and work out how your time has been divided between work, family and God. After the review, plan your forward diary for the next year, making sure it reflects your chosen lifestyle and priorities. Within this forward plan, make sure you allow for flexibility. Schedule some 'spare' time, in case the unexpected happens.

NOTES

HOMEWORK /GOING DEEPER

Use the blank pie-chart to plot an estimate of how much time you have spent on work, with your family and with God/church over the last year. An example is filled in to show you what to do. Then consider what you would like the trend lines to be.

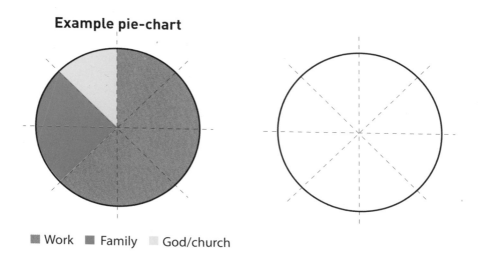

Example pie-chart

■ Work ■ Family ▨ God/church

Spend some more time praying about the right priorities for your life. Conduct an official diary review and prayerfully plan your diary for the next year, ensuring it reflects your future priorities.

VERSES FOR MEDITATION IN TIMES OF STRESS

Psalm 46

Isaiah 43:1-3

Matthew 6:25-34

Philippians 4:6-7

SESSION 5

Failure, Disappointment and Hope

EXERCISE 1: FAILURE

Share your own experience of failure or disappointment in the workplace with those in your group.

FAITH AND ETERNITY

Christian hope: the knowledge that we are made by a God who loves each one of us.

'And hope does not disappoint us, because God has poured out his love into our hearts by the Holy Spirit, whom he has given us' (Romans 5:5).

FORGIVENESS AND RESTORING RELATIONSHIPS

Build good relationships with colleagues. '...live at peace with everyone' (Romans 12:18).

Be people of:
- Grace
- Truth
- Trust

REBUILDING TRUST

- Grace from God
- Approach other person
- Apologise
- Forgive and move on

EXERCISE 2: IDENTIFYING BROKEN TRUST

Ask yourself the following questions in relation to your current work situation and then share your answers with your small group. (There will be time to pray through any issues that arise at the end of the session.)

- what have I failed to do that I should be doing?
- what have I done (or am I doing) that I should not do?
- what has the other person done, or failed to do?
- what has been said that has been hurtful?

EXERCISE 3: LEARNING FROM FAILURE

This exercise is an opportunity to list any recent failures at work and assess what we can learn from them, as well as what could be done differently next time. Fill in the table below, listing any recent failures. Write your responses to the questions in the table.

Failure	What can I learn from it?	What would I do differently next time?

PAIN

What can it tell us?

FAILURE – AN OPPORTUNITY TO GROW!

We are only failures if Christ fails in us – and he will never do that.

'...he who began a good work in you will carry it on to completion' (Philippians 1:6).

Acknowledge our failures and learn from them.

John 21, the disciples and the catch of fish.

God promises to work in all things for the good of those who love him (Romans 8:28).

NOTES

_____

_____

_____

_____

_____

_____

_____

_____

HOW TO RECOVER AND RENEW OUR HOPE

'Some name it disappointment and become poorer, others name it experience and become richer' (Siegmund Warburg).

FIVE STEPS TO RENEW HOPE

1. TURN TO GOD (RATHER THAN IMPLICATE HIM IN THE FAILURE)

Disciples on road to Emmaus were so preoccupied with disappointment they failed to recognise the Lord of hope walking alongside them.

Jesus has promised never to abandon us (Matthew 28:20).

2. FACE THE FACTS, YET STILL BELIEVE

Abraham and Sarah longed for a child. Abraham acknowledges how old he and Sarah are, yet he still trusted in God's promise (Romans 4:19).

3. MEDITATE ON SCRIPTURE LED BY THE SPIRIT

Meditating on his word helps reinforce our hope (Romans 15:13).

4. KEEP A JOURNAL

Record prayers and thoughts. Review regularly.

5. PERSEVERE IN HOPE

'...suffering produces perseverance; perseverance, character; and character, hope' (Romans 5:2-4).

HOMEWORK/ GOING DEEPER

Take some time to pray into any relationships at work where you know that forgiveness is required. Either alone, or with other members of the group, spend some time forgiving those people before God, and asking forgiveness for your part (if any) in the difficulty. Pray for God's blessing on all your work relationships going forward.

NOTES

SESSION 6

Money and Giving

A biblical view of money and giving.

EXERCISE 1

From largest to smallest, list the areas where your money goes. Look at where giving to God and the church come in the list.

Do you think this should be higher up?

Discuss your findings and your answers to the questions with your small group.

WHAT IS MONEY FOR?

Primarily a medium of exchange.

Also:
- A store of value (eg, savings)
- A vehicle of blessing:
  > The receiver and the giver
  > Christian duty to the poor/ social justice
- A test of stewardship
- A means of worshipping God
- Testimony and witnessing about God
- For making friends (Luke 16:9) by investing in people and relationships
- For investing in the Kingdom of God (1 Timothy 6:19)

'You eat, but never have enough. You drink, but never have your fill. You put on clothes, but are not warm. You earn wages, only to put them in a purse with holes in it' (Haggai 1:6).

JESUS OR MONEY – WHO WILL BE THE MASTER?

'You cannot serve both God and money' (Luke 16:13).

'The worker deserves his wages' (Luke 10:7).

'The love of money is a root of all kinds of evil' (1 Timothy 6:9-10).

EXERCISE 2: SELF SEEKING OR SEEKING SENSE?

In small groups, read through the table below together.

Look at the four key distinctions between self seeking and seeking sense and discuss the differences between the two.

Self Seeking	Seeking Sense
Exclusive (Thinks of self at exclusion of others)	Inclusive (Thinking of self doesn't exclude thinking of others)
Excessive (Tendency to always want more)	Sufficient (Desires not necessarily excessive)
Restrictive (Finds it difficult to give)	Releasing (Giving may come easily)
Stifling (Finds it hard when others prosper)	Empowering (May help others to prosper)

If we find giving difficult, rather than joyful, then money may have become our master.

GREED OR GENEROSITY – HOW DO WE DEAL WITH MONEY?

1. Handle small amounts properly and you will be trusted with more (Luke 16:10-11)
2. If you cannot handle money properly, who will trust you with true riches?

DUTY AND PRIVILEGE – WHY DO WE GIVE?

- Grace

- Faith
  'For great is the Lord and most worthy of praise; he is to be feared above all gods' (Psalm 96:4)

- Blessing
  'Test me and see if I don't open up heaven itself to you and pour out blessings beyond your wildest dreams' (Malachi 3:10, The Message)

WHAT SHOULD GIVING LOOK LIKE?

1. CELEBRATION

A celebration of what we have been given from God.

Paul says, 'Because of the service by which you have proved yourselves, people will praise God' (2 Corinthians 9:13)

'God loves a cheerful giver' (2 Corinthians 9:7)

2. FREEDOM

We will be possessed by that which we cannot give freely.

Giving is the antidote to materialism.

3. INVESTMENT

i) In our relationship with God (2 Corinthians 9:10)
ii) In God's wider kingdom (Philippians 4:17-18)

SMALL GROUP DISCUSSION

Identify work in your church which excites you and that you would like to invest in. Discuss your response with your small group.

THE PRACTICALITIES OF GIVING

AS A HABIT

Make a start.

'Give and it will be given to you... For the measure you use, it will be measured to you' (Luke 6:38).

TO WHOM SHOULD WE GIVE?

The lion's share should go to the church.

HOW SHOULD WE GIVE?

Giving should usually be anonymous, the left hand should

not know what the right hand is doing (Matthew 6:3).

Not just money – time, skills, possessions, etc, through volunteering at the church. Insure someone else to drive our car.

WHEN SHOULD WE GIVE?

The Bible encourages regular giving (1 Corinthians 16:2).

WHAT SHOULD WE GIVE?

New Testament focuses on our attitude rather than the quantity.

EXERCISE 3: WHAT CAN WE GIVE?

List what you feel you should/can give in terms of your time/possessions/skills, etc. Share what you have written with your small groups. Pray for each other, that you would have the grace to be generous givers and give as God guides you to.

DEBT

Get out of debt quickly. Talk to someone about the problem and make a plan.

RESPONSIBLE ENJOYMENT OF POSSESSIONS

Giving frees us up to enjoy God's goodness precisely because our priorities are right. When we have the balance right, we'll be able to enjoy both what we have and what we give.

NOTES

_____

_____

_____

_____

_____

_____

_____

_____

_____

_____

_____

_____

_____

HOMEWORK/GOING DEEPER

The following exercises can be used to go deeper in this issue.

ASSESS YOUR GIVING EXERCISE

Take some time to re-assess your giving in terms of who, how, when and what. Imagine the blank pie-charts in your manual represent all the money and time that you give in a year. Divide up the pie-charts as you would like to divide up your giving. Adjust any plans to give in the light of this.

DIVIDING UP YOUR GIVING

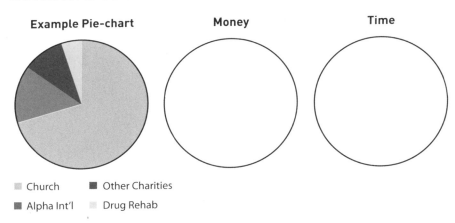

Example Pie-chart **Money** **Time**

Church   Other Charities
Alpha Int'l   Drug Rehab

THE 'SIX MONTH CHALLENGE'

Suggest growing in faith-based giving by taking up a six month challenge of either:

1. Reducing your discretionary spending by X%;

2. Increasing your giving by X%, or

3. Matching your luxury spending with equal giving (eg, if you buy a treat for yourself, give the equivalent amount away)

At the end of the six months meet together again in your small group to discuss what God has done in your lives over that period.

FURTHER INFORMATION

For further information about *God at Work* please see: godatwork.org

> **We would love to hear your feedback on the course. Please tell us your thoughts online at: godatwork.org.uk**

For the complete list of *God at Work* podcasts, please see: godatwork.org.uk/podcast

Alpha International publishes a wide range of resources for many different ministries. One of these ministries, Alpha in the Workplace, has developed a version of the Alpha course designed for use in a workplace setting. To learn more about this course, or to find out how to run one in your own workplace, please visit alpha.org/workplace

To find out more about the Alpha course, or to find a course near you, please visit alpha.org or alphafriends.org

To order *God at Work* resources, or any other Alpha International products, please visit:

- alphashop.org
- call the Alpha Publications Hotline on 0845 7581 278
- email alpha@stl.org
- to order products from overseas, please call + 44 1228 611 749